Presented
To

_____

From

_____

World History in Verse

Volume 1 – Old Testament and Ancient Egypt

with Professor Archie Ology

Written and Illustrated
By David Manley

Special thanks to:

Micah Olson
For the digitzing,
painstaking technical layout expertise
and friendship.

Published By
Line Upon Line Productions
Accent Digital Publishing
accentdigitalpublishing.com
Copyright © 2010
All Rights Reserved

ISBN 978-1-60445-0682

To Julie...
after all, it has been
your vision all along,
as you have been mine.

History

History's like a river with
beginning and an end
lending us perspective to
look back from every bend;

        starting high on Eden's slope
           and trickling to a fall,
    then to the East it wandered with
           a sad and lonely call.

It gathered force and multiplied
into a mighty flood
that buried memories but left
their stories in the mud;

    and when the tide subsided all
        was clean and pure again,
  and streams woke up and traveled
    with the wayward maps of men.

They eddied 'round the thrones of kings
and furrowed valley floors,
fed the kingdoms, filled the barns
with precious living stores;

carried off adventurers
taught the trades they plied,
merged the many rivulets,
mixed the culture's pride.

The river mined for metals, and it
dug up costly stones,
set up monuments to men
but bleached their feeble bones.

History logs the glory that
mankind has lost and won,
a river that defines just how
we've turned from God and run.

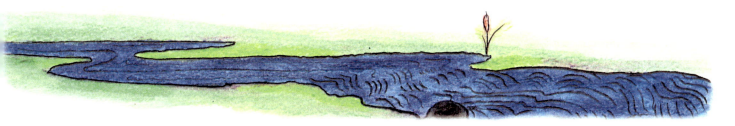

Contents

All Aboard!

Every look at ancient times
is like a search for treasure
'cause digging up the artifacts
of hist'ry is a pleasure!

An archeologist is one
who learns to read the clues
and re-creates the stories that
our memories will lose.

This trip down through time begins
as God's creating Earth,
and it ends with Romans de-
monstrating all their worth.

Serving as your guide today,
we introduce the wise
Professor Archie Ology
(who wears the neatest ties).

You can help the good Professor
keep track of his duckie
so he won't have lost it by
the ending if we're lucky.

Now prepare to turn the pages,
listen close and look,
and enjoy the rhyming verses
offered in this book.

Creation

It took a day to make the Day
and sep'rate it from Night;

    it took a second the way God reckoned
    to give the heav'ns their height;

the third was spent as oceans lent
the dirt a place to dry,
and grass and weeds sprung up from seeds
and fruit grew low and high;

    the fourth got baked, the sun awake'd
    and climbed to catch the moon
    then went to bed, but God had said
    be back each day by noon;

and with His words God made the birds
and fishes on the fifth;
He stocked the creeks and made the beaks
the warblers warble with;

the sixth was when God fashioned men
and all the other creatures,
legs and hair and each in pair
with reproductive features;

and when the fun was finally done,
God thought He needed rest,
and since that time new parents find
a nap helps out the best.

Sin

We were made to trust our Maker,
like a puppy does his BOY,
to be dazzled by God's bigness,
by his love, and constant joy.
We were made to romp together
and explore inviting canyons
in adventures great and small,
best of friends, and true companions.
But one day we wandered on
after Master told us, "Stay!"
and we found a coiled snake
full of poison in our way.

SUDDENLY, its painful bite
sent us yipping down the trail;
full of fear and guilt we ran
tucking in our puppy tail.
Then, to make it worse, we hid
from our Master, good and wise,
hid in painful shame believing
He'd have anger in His eyes.
After all, we'd disobeyed Him
and deserved His righteous wrath;
we just didn't understand
that He missed us on the path.

GOD HAS AN ANTIDOTE FOR SNAKE POISON.
DO YOU KNOW WHAT IT IS?
READ ROMANS 6:23

SNAKE BITE

3

Leaves

After disobeying God,
Adam found out he was bare
so he went and picked some leaves,
sewed them in a skirt to wear.

But the problem with some leaves
is they shrivel up and dry;
Adam couldn't hide his guilt;
Adam had begun to die.

Leaves become a picture of
our attempts to hide our sin.
God, it took, to make our Cover
with His sacrificial skin.

4

Early Inhabitants

Though, doubtless, men have lived in caves,
we do not come from cavemen;
nor were we born in cosmic goo,
but fully grown in Eden.

The people weren't hunched over and
real hairy like the apes;
we weren't evolving animals
with minds the size of grapes.

No, men who first walked on the Earth
were tall and big and strong,
were healthy and majestic, and
they lived extremely long.

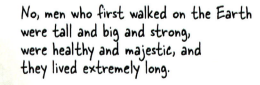

But, packaged with a glory that
the angels even wanted,
the people became proud and mean
with selfishness they flaunted.

They cheated, robbed, and made up lies,
they fought and killed for fun
until our good Creator had
to stop what they'd begun.

It grieved Him deeply in His heart,
but He devised a plan
to end their wickedness and start
again with just one man.

He found a servant who alone
found favor in His sight,
a preacher who would warn the others
of their dreadful plight.

And with this righteous man He shared
His plans to save the Earth
preserving everything alive,
to God, the greatest worth.

God loved the creatures of His world,
He loved His image there--
the man and woman and the children
coming from the pair.

Sadly, He would use a flood
to wash our early stain
teaching us that selfish pride
can only end in pain.

And when the rainbow comes we hear
God reassuring Man
that kindness and relationship
have always been His plan.

Noah

Noah built a boat
so that he could float.
All were safe inside,
though it was a ride.
When the land had dried,
Noah knelt and cried.
God gave him a note
with a rainbow wrote.
We can read it still,
learn about His will
'cause He doesn't change
tho' we rearrange.

NOAH'S FAMILY AND ALL THE ANIMALS
LIVED IN THE ARK OVER A YEAR!

Babel

When Noah's grown-up children
fin'lly dried off all the mud,
they multiplied and soon forgot
the reason for the flood.
Their sinful hearts grew darker
as they hid and turned away;
they started to imagine things
that led them far astray.
People got the notion they
could fight the very God
who mixed the clay, then gave His breath
to make them living sod.
They thought together they had power,
searching far and wide
for a place to build a tower
that would symbolize their pride.
Well, talk about a mixed-up mess
of foolishness infused,
it's not a wonder that God couldn't
leave them all confused.

BABYLONIAN ZIGGURAT OF UR

THERE ARE OVER 6900 LANGUAGES IN THE WORLD. GOD SPEAKES THEM ALL FLUENTLY!

He talked about it with Himself
 deciding to come down
  to save them from their silly talk
  and scatter them around.
  He mixed up all their languages
   and sent them wand'ring off––
    but men still didn't learn we speak
    to praise and not to scoff.
    So sadly as the story goes,
     the nations grew up lost,
      never comprehending what
       their sin would really cost.
        Now though that tower's disappeared,
         a broken monument,
          we're apt to miss God's message there,
         to miss His heart's intent––
        Today our many languages
         show infinite design
       and point to Him, the Word that speaks,
        a hanging welcome sign.

WELCOME

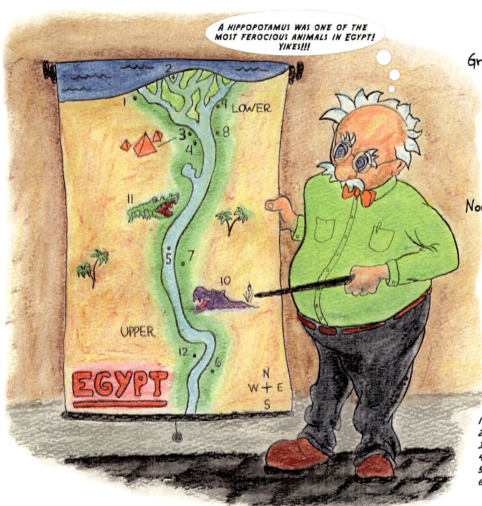

Egypt

Groups of people scattered and they
found the fertile Nile;
towns sprung up along its banks
mile after mile.
Local governments would form,
sep'rate kingdoms rose;
rulers came to make up laws
and to watch for foes.
Nomads parked their camels and they
started farming there;
builders, bakers, teachers came
trading for their fare.
People searching for a life
found a lush frontier;
Egypt became populated
all the Nile near.

1 ALEXADRIA   7 AMARNA
2 ROSETTA   8 CAIRO
3 GIZA   9 AVARIS
4 MEMPHIS   10 HIPPOPOTOMUS
5 NILE   11 CROCODILE
6 THEBES   12 VALLEY OF THE KINGS

The river cooled the desert heat
and made the mud for bricks;
it let the workmen splash and drink
pausing with their picks.
Logs and stones were floated up
from forests in the South;
river boats with traders plied
from mountains to the mouth.
All along the reeds would churn
with crocodile's swish;
all along the children played
and hoped to catch a fish.
Swelling when the mountain rains
sent cascading floods;
growing grass where cattle grazed
and slowly chewed their cuds.

TEMPLE OF PHILIA

Egypt was a lovely place
but disregarded truth;
strange beliefs about their kings
distorted it from youth.
People had begun to think
their rulers were divine,
and they worshipped them as gods
right down through the line.
Still our good Creator waited
patiently with grace
anticipating soon a time
when He would show His place.

ANUBIS: GOD OF THE UNDERWORLD

RAMSES II

Menes

Menes was an early king,
a man with just one head,
but he wore a double crown,
a white one, and a red.

The white one pictured upper Egypt
which was in the South,
the red one, for the northern ground
around the Nile's mouth.

Menes fought to unify
both these separate lands
making people live together
under his commands.

LOWER
-NORTH-

UPPER
-SOUTH-

MENES IS PRONOUNCED MEE-NEEZ

14

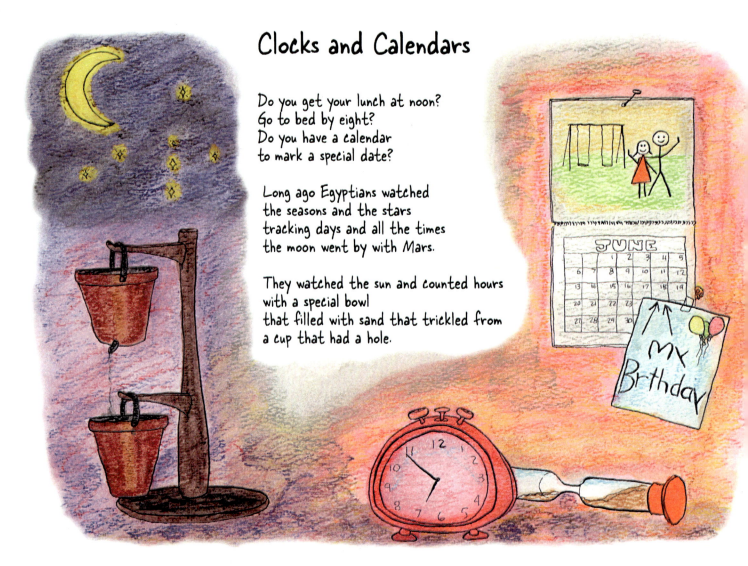

Clocks and Calendars

Do you get your lunch at noon?
Go to bed by eight?
Do you have a calendar
to mark a special date?

Long ago Egyptians watched
the seasons and the stars
tracking days and all the times
the moon went by with Mars.

They watched the sun and counted hours
with a special bowl
that filled with sand that trickled from
a cup that had a hole.

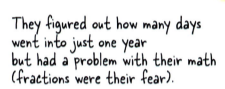

They figured out how many days
went into just one year
but had a problem with their math
(fractions were their fear).

Eventually their seasons would get
mixed-up and reversed;
their calendar be backwards with
their ending months the first!

I wish they could have figured out
to add an extra day
for every four years that go by
just like we do today.

Hieroglyphics

Pencils weren't invented yet,
and neither were computers;
mailmen never brought the maidens
letters from their suitors.

  People back in Egypt didn't
  have an alphabet;
  so, instead, they made up pictures
  for the words they set.

A duck they might have drawn like this,
a fish was really easy,
a summer day would show the sun,
but lines would make it breezy.

  Of course, it would be difficult
  to write about a pizza
  'specially if you wanted one
  with lots of different meatsa.

The pictures also stood for sounds,
a study we call phonics;
today we're thankful for the help
we get from electronics.

Languages are difficult
to learn no matter what;
learning how to write a sound
can really crack your nut.

Hieroglyphics took a student
many years to learn;
children who became a scribe
had to wait their turn.

Papyrus

Paper comes from trees, we know,
not too unlike long ago
when the people gathered REEDS
from the marshy Nile weeds.
Watching close for crocodiles
they would cut and stack up piles
which were peeled and laid in strips,
layered so there were no rips,
beaten flat into a sheet,
dried beneath the desert heat,
glued together in a roll,
'til they had a perfect scroll.

PAPYRUS PLANT

Then the scribes could write their letters
using sticks or pointy feathers
which they dipped in special ink
black or red (and maybe pink).

Since papyrus was real tough,
people never got enough;
they could weave it into cloth,
cook it in a tasty broth;
they could make some shoes or hats,
braid it into sleeping mats,
make a sail or length of rope,
tie a cage or envelope.
All in all, papyrus was
popular for all it does.

SCROLLS WERE EASIER TO USE BUT
STONE CARVINGS ARE WHAT LAST!

Sumer

"Sumer" rhymes with "rumor,"
    a really famous place,
    where ancient people lived
    who were a pagan race.

We can find their treasures
    when digging in the sand
    and think the town of Ur
    was in this fertile land.

Today it's called, "Iraq,"
    and very far away,
but must have been where Abraham
    was born and learned to play.

Abraham

Abraham did not believe
just everything he heard,
but was a man who DID BELIEVE
when God gave him His word.

It's kind of like you do when mom
has promised to make lunch;
you assume it will appear
when its time to munch.

Faith is simply trusting
that God will follow through
if He came and promised He
would take you to the zoo.

God made Abraham a father;
we become his kin
the moment we believe that Jesus
takes away our sin.

GOD MAKES REALLY NEAT PROMISES
FOR US TO BELIEVE. TWO ARE FOUND IN
JOHN 3:16 AND HEBREWS 13:5!

ABRAHAM'S DEPARTURE
BY JÓZSEF MOLNÁR

Covenant

A covenant's a special promise
you would make your bud,
but something so important you
would sign it with your blood.
It tells him you will always keep
your end of the deal
no matter what the cost and
no matter what you feel.

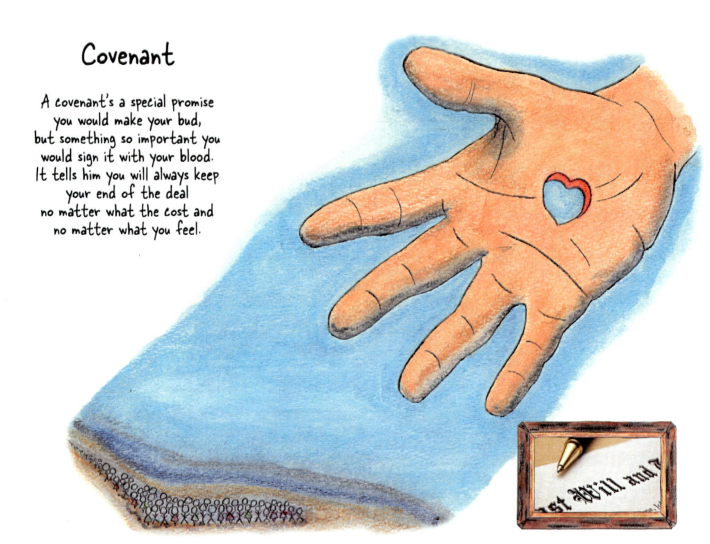

God has made a few of these
with people of the past,
with Noah, and with Abraham,
with Israel to last.
But the greatest covenant
coming from above
is the promise Jesus made
of eternal love.
When we have communion, we
renew this precious pact
remembering His blood supplies
life that we had lacked.

DESTRUCTION OF SODOM AND GOMORRAH
BY JOHN MARTIN

Sodom

Sodom was a city
of people who were bad,
people mean and selfish
who made God really sad.

Lot lived in this city
with his family, too,
but angels came and warned him
to leave with those he knew.

In His mercy, God
decided He would end
Sodom's misery
with fire He would send.

Lot snatched up his fam'ly
and barely made it out,
the angels telling them
not to look or pout.

And then a blazing fire
fell upon the city,
leaving in the ashes
all that had been pretty.

Mrs. Lot looked back
and by the charcoal stayed,
turned into a statue
because she disobeyed.

Isaac

Isaac was a miracle
like every baby is,
but Isaac had a special purpose
that alone was his.
For just a moment he became
a sacrificial lamb
when bound below his father's knife
before they saw the ram.
Isaac got to make a picture
as a little boy
of our Father's sacrifice
to bring us lasting joy.

JESUS WAS THE REAL SACRIFICE ISAAC PICTURED. WE CAN SHOW OUR THANKFULNESS BY BEING KIND AND HELPFUL TO OTHERS!

SACRIFICE OF ISAAC
BY LAURENT DE LA HIRE

26

Joseph

Jacob became Israel
  and had a bunch of boys;
    12 around the dinner table
      make a lot of noise!

Joseph was a younger one,
  a favorite of his dad,
    which made his older brothers really
      jealous, really mad.

They pretended Joseph died
  and hid him in a cave;
    and when some foreign traders passed,
      they sold him as a slave!

BY HIS TRUST, JOSEPH GOT TO SHOW EVERYONE HOW GOOD GOD WAS.

WHEAT BERRIES

DATES

Down in Egypt Joseph trusted
 God knew where he stood;
  what his brothers meant for evil,
   God had meant for good.

Soon a famine would be coming;
 it would take a man
  who wisely sought the heart of God
   to come up with a plan.

To save that heathen nation
 and save his family, too,
  Joseph testified to Pharaoh
   of the God he knew.

Then he got to work as
 the second-in-command;
  right below the king, Joseph
   ruled that ancient land.

28

Hammurabi

Hammurabi was a king
ruling ancient Babylon
known for all the laws he made
lasting still though he is gone.
While the Hebrews lived in Egypt,
after Abraham had died,
after Joseph came and went,
but before the law applied,

Hammurabi made decrees
for his Fertile Crescent valleys
carried by his traders east,
west on shipping routes by galleys.
Tablets from old Babylon
tell of industry and science,
mathematics, medicine,
ways a king enforced compliance,
how to traffic human slaves,
edicts for inheritance,
standard prices for a wife,
rules for debts with deference.

HAMMURABI

29

This and more is locked up safe
in museums' vaulted fill
with the Code of Hammurabi
lingering a reference still.
Bless'd, however, is the man
who delights in God's own law
meditating on it 'til
getting it into his craw.

CODE OF HAMMURABI

Mummy

Egyptians didn't want to die;
they thought another life
awaited them beyond the grave
without pain and strife.

They thought that in this other world
when people woke, alive,
they'd need their body and some food
to walk around and thrive.

And since Egyptians thought like this,
they tried to find a way
to save a person's body after
he had passed away.

At first they buried corpses
in shallow desert pits
which dried the bodies so they didn't
crumble into bits;

but then the jackals dug them up
and scattered them around
which made them much too difficult
by spirits to be found.

ANUBIS WITH MUMMY

Someone then thought up a plan
to use a wooden coffin
which helped to keep the body safe
and helped its trip to soften;

BUT the problem with a coffin
is that air gets in,
and, with air, the bodies rot
and decompose within.

Rotten bodies were no good
for spirits needing parts,
and so some people still alive
learned embalming arts.

They would lay a body out
and make some special cuts
which would let them reach inside
and pull out all the guts.

BLACK BACKED JACKAL

JACKAL FROM TUT'S TOOMB

32

Brains were scooped out with a spoon
or sucked out through the nose;
it really is a shame that they weren't
packed in ice and froze.

The body then was dried with salts
and rubbed with different lotions;
the people took real serious
these resurrection notions.

After many days the corpse
was stuffed to keep its shape,
then wrapped with strips of linen like
we wrap a bat with tape.

HOWARD CARTER EXAMINING
KING TUT'S MUMMY

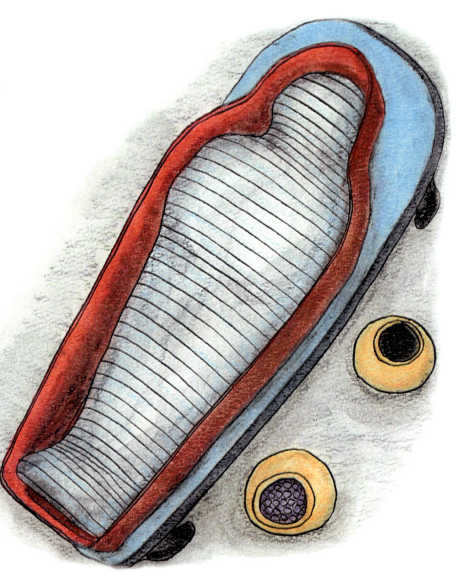

PEOPLE WHO DON'T KNOW THE TRUTH
SURE COME UP WITH STRANGE IDEAS!

The whole thing then was coated with
a salty resin pitch
and put inside a casket that
was gold if they'd been rich.

These could last for many years,
thousands we are told,
'cause scientists have messed around
with specimens that old.

Bodies that are saved like this
would make an awful tent;
can you picture moving in
if it was for rent?

I admit this topic makes
me queasy in my tummy—
ancients called it "momia,"
we call it a mummy.

MUMMY IN THE
VATICAN MUSEUM

34

Pyramids

Pyramids were made with rocks
cut in big and heavy blocks;
square and tight was every joint
rising up into a point.

One by one, the layers filled,
taking many years to build.
Workers would get really hot;
and the big ones cost a lot!

Mostly they were giant tombs
and they hid these secret rooms
full of gold and swords and bones,
treasure from Egyptian thrones.

If you'd like to try and make one,
using sugar cubes is fun;
you could stack and paint them yellow
then re-use them in some jello.

ONE BLOCK USED IN THE PYRAMIDS COULD WEIGH AS MUCH AS A MINIVAN!

CANOPIC JARS CONTAINING MUMMIFIED ORGANS

KING TUTANKHAMUN'S BURIAL MASK

Afterlife

If you thought your fun in heaven
depended on the things you brought,
I imagine all your pockets
would be full of things you bought.
If you could bring toys and snacks,
color crayons, videos,
if you could bring animals
or some polish for your toes,
I imagine you would want
all the things that you could pack,
all the things you really loved,
or could fit into a sack.

TREASURES FROM
EGYPTIAN TOMBS

36

I think you would die prepared
if your comfort was your goal--
so the rich Egyptian people
tried to bring things for their soul.
Back then no one understood
we can't bring things when we're dead;

treasure from this life remains,
but we can send some ahead.
Jesus tells us pile up
riches that will always last
by the good things that we do
when our life has finally passed.

MANY CULTURES IMAGINE LIFE AFTER DEATH. WHAT DO YOU THINK IT WILL BE LIKE?

Hyksos

Hyksos came down from the North
taking Egypt by surprise;
chariots, their secret weapon,
conquering with greedy eyes.

Avaris, their capitol,
in the Nile Delta plain
choosing it instead of Thebes
as the spot from which they'd reign.

For one-hundred fifty years
these usurpers kept the throne;
Pharaoh Ahmose drove them out
finally taking back the loan.

ANCIENT EGYPTIAN CHARIOT

MOSES HAD TO LEARN TO DO THINGS GOD'S WAY. HAVE YOU LEARNED THAT?

Moses

Moses was a little brother
born in very dangerous times,
put into a floating basket
waterproofed with tarry slimes.
Found, an orphan, by a princess
and adopted as her son,
he became a prince of Egypt,
Hebrew lineage known to none.
As a man of forty years
he began to sense a need,
to defend his Jewish brothers
so they wouldn't strain and bleed.
But his anger, uncontrolled,
flared up, and a life he took;
for the murder, had to flee
picking up a shepherd's crook.

THE FINDING OF MOSES
BY LAWRENCE ALMA-TADEMA

39

As a man of eighty years,
at the timing of God's choice,
he returned to Egypt sure
that he'd learned to hear God's voice.
With a mighty show of magic
from some power God supplied,
Moses led his people out
while Egyptians 'round them died.
After many years in Egypt
Israel was headed home
as a giant family now,
though they slowly had to roam.
And for all the journey Moses
taught the people how to hear,
showing them how God desired
in His love to draw them near.

MOSES BEFORE THE BURNING BUSH
DOMENICO FETTI

40

10 Commandments

God's a Teacher with a file
of commandments to be blessed
that He told us we must follow
or we'd fail to pass His test.

First, we must believe that He
was and is the only God;

    second, we were not to carve
    images; they're always flawed;

third, we weren't to say His name
uselessly or without love;

    fourth, we need remember how
    Sabbath rest is from above;

fifth, we always are to treat
parents really, really nice;

sixth, He told us murder's not
   an option, but a wicked vice;

seventh, made our secret parts
to be shared with just our spouse;

   eighth, He told us not to steal
      someone's mansion or his mouse;

ninth, we learned we couldn't lie
since it hurts our Godly neighbor;

   tenth, we weren't to covet but
      to seek for blessing from our labor.

BY REMBRANDT

These commandments we each break;
   they're a test that we all fail,
   and for flunking we deserve
      to be thrown away in jail;

   but our Teacher's really smart,
   sends a Letter in the mail—
   new instructions how to pass
      that got tacked up with a nail.

gods

Ancient cultures strangely thought
many gods existed;
spirits that could take on human
forms were often listed.
Egyptian stories tell of spirits,
strange but somehow strong,
wanting worship from the people--
what they did was wrong.

   Hapi was their water god
     who Moses turned to blood;
Heket was a goddess frog
who multiplied in mud;
    Geb was known the god of dust,
     who Moses turned to lice;
Kepri, pictured as a fly,
was unique, but not nice;
    Hathor was their god of love,
     her head just like a cow's;

HATHOR

ISIS

43

THANK YOU, GOD, FOR BEING GOOD AND FOR TELLING US THE TRUTH.

HORUS

Isis, god of medicine,
with boils did arouse;
    Nut, their goddess of the sky,
    was crushed with giant hail;
Seth, their god of blowing storms,
the locust hoards would flail;
    Ra, the sun, a mighty god,
    for three days in the dark;
even Pharaoh's oldest son,
a "god," looked like a lark.

gods, aside from Yahweh, are
rude and always fake;
they lie and cheat and hurt Mankind
with everything they take.
gods like these are enemies
deceiving with their lies,
but Jesus has defeated them
His blood, our freedom buys.

Pharaohs

Egypt's gone through many rulers;
dynasties were passing down
from a father to his son
power with the royal crown.

PHARAOHS WEREN'T ELECTED. MOST RULED BECAUSE THEIR FATHER RULED BEFORE THEM... UNTIL SOMEONE STRONGER FORCED THEM OUT.

Some were strong and some were weak,
some were cruel and really low,
some built things that last today;
most we hardly even know.
Pharaoh Thutmose led his army
farther north than any other,
and Hatshepsut was his daughter;
Moses might have called her mother.

HATSHEPSUT

TUTANKHAMUN

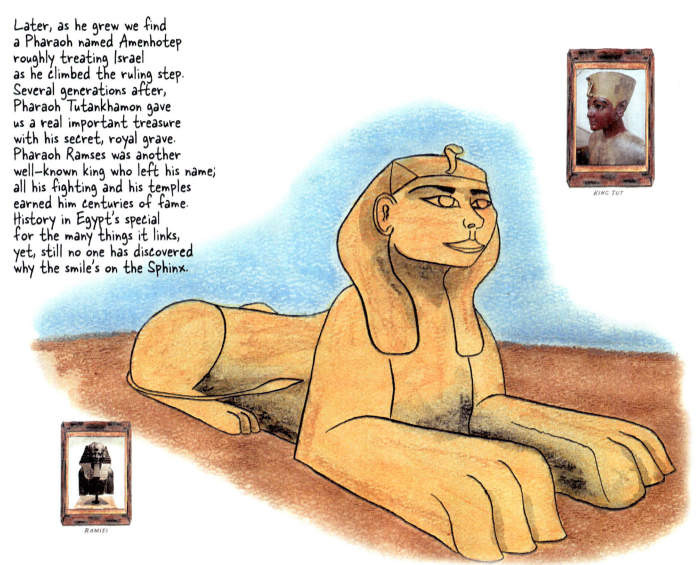

Later, as he grew we find
a Pharaoh named Amenhotep
roughly treating Israel
as he climbed the ruling step.
Several generations after,
Pharaoh Tutankhamon gave
us a real important treasure
with his secret, royal grave.
Pharaoh Ramses was another
well—known king who left his name;
all his fighting and his temples
earned him centuries of fame.
History in Egypt's special
for the many things it links,
yet, still no one has discovered
why the smile's on the Sphinx.

KING TUT

RAMSES

46

Rosetta Stone

Rosetta is a town in Egypt
where some soldiers found
a rock with words all over it;
they dug it from the ground.
The words were carved into the stone,
but no one understood
the language that was really old,
a mystery, it stood.
Some they knew were hieroglyphics,
some were ancient Greek,
others were a Coptic language
commoners would speak.

Then in 1822,
one man cracked the code,
Jean-François Champollion
hit the mother-lode!
Finally understanding that
the pictures stood for sounds,
Jean-François was like a hunter
on a scent with hounds.
Slowly all the little carvings
started to make sense
since he could contrast the different
languages and tense.
And since his discovery,
scholars have been able
to read Egyptian writings whether
story, law, or label.

Kings

Israel wanted to try it
under a threat of a riot,
but they found out what kings were about
and, quickly, regretted their diet.

THE BOOKS OF 1ST AND 2ND KINGS TELL OF ISRAEL'S RULERS, MOST OF WHOM WEREN'T GOOD.

Alexander

Alexander was "the Great"
if warfare is what matters
and, certainly, all earthly wealth
was brought to him on platters;
a Greek from Macedonia,
defeating Persian rule,
he taught the world his lessons like
a teacher does at school.
He brought along his architects
and Hellenistic culture,
gathering the kingdoms like
a young and greedy vulture.
Relatively quickly, he
had conquered all the places
that were known with glory and
subdued their many races.
Even Egypt bears his mark
and was a land to tame—
it still contains a city titled
after him by name.

HELLENISTIC REFERS TO GREEK ORIGIN

Rome

Rome is built on seven hills,
a city very famous,
named after a pair of brothers,
Romulus and Remus.
First, as a republic, Romans
shared their government;
everybody voting
by the local people sent.

ROMAN STATUE

But as happens everywhere,
power fell to greed;
one man rose to take control,
an Emperor to lead!
Caesar was his name, but
the word became a title
for the man who ruled the nations
with his will their bridle.

WOLF NURSING TWINS

AQUEDUCT

ROMAN CIVILIZATION LASTED HUNDREDS OF YEARS, AND IT'S NETWORK WAS A TOOL GOD USED TO SPREAD THE GOOD NEWS ABOUT JESUS!

Building roads to travel faster,
armies raced around
with their weapons threatening
and keeping people bound.
Like the Pharaohs, Caesars made
the people worship them,
forcing adoration like
a counterfeited gem;

craving greater glory and
coveting man's praise,
Caesars tried to steal what was
God's in wicked ways.
But like Egypt figured out,
like Persia, and like Greece,
Rome would soon discover that
power's on a lease.

PANTHEON

52

Names

Down through time come famous stories,
warriors and victories,
names of mystery and awe,
names of special strength and power--

Nimrod with his might, and tall
Orion hung up in the sky,
Theseus, and Hercules,

Ozymandias, the King,
Ulysses, brave, and Don Quixote,
Ramses, and Napoleon,

William Wallace, Peter Pan,
Alexander, Julius,
Roland, Arthur, Darius,
Robin Hood, and Beowulf,
Israel, and Marco Polo,
Obadiah, Genghis Khan,
Ruth, and Esther, Washington,

Jason, Atlas, Gilgamesh,
Eric, James, and Cleopatra,
Samson, Daniel, and Elijah,
Uzza, George, and Hammurabi,
Solomon, and Constantine--

hunters and adventurers,
rulers, emperors, and kings,
vikings, pirates, buccaneers,
warriors and famous all;
fact or fiction, myth and tale,
on and on the list can stretch,
each one leaving just a story,
each one leaving just a name.

Every name lacks but a body
every name, that is, **but one**;
all succumb to death and fading,
all succumb, that is, **but one**.

I BET YOU KNOW WHO THAT ONE IS!

Names of figures on credits page

B.C.

Though we must extrapolate,
records seem to indicate
people scattered all directions
from the fertile crescent sections.
North to Turkey, round to Europe,
staying in the field and stirrup;
Eastward Asian peoples went,
China and the orient.

South to Africa and West,
looking forward, on they pressed,
stopping here and there to build
homes amidst the valleys tilled.
Pilgrims each one in our race,
all this travel taking place
four millennia before
Jesus came to fix the score.

Egypt's oldest kingdoms date
around 3098.
Abraham began his line
around 2069.
1898 was when
Joseph came with brothers ten.
Seventeen and eighty-four
Hammurabi paced the floor.
1600's, Hyksos came,
Asians taking Egypt's fame.

Pharaoh Ahmose kicked them out
snatching back Egyptian clout.
Thutmose and Amenhotep
later climbed the ruling step
making slaves of Israelites
'til God's people had no rights.
Around 1525
Moses might have been alive,
and by 1446
Israel made no more bricks.

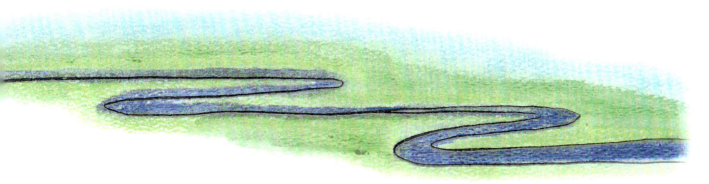

Judges in the promised land
helped the people understand
how they might inherit blessing
tho' their foes around were pressing.
While the heathen nations fumbled,
God would speak through people humbled
dwelling near them in a tent,
closer to His first intent.

By 1000 David showed
that the heart was God's abode,
but the Hebrew kings that followed
languished, in their sin they wallowed;
all the worse for knowing better
bound, again, with sin their fetter;
crying out and being saved,
freedom real they deeply craved.

Babylon and Persia came
conquering and taking fame.
Alexander, down from Greece
fought to hold the world in peace.
Finally, Rome came with her hoards,
building roads, and swinging swords:
emperors and kingdoms passed;
some were small and some were vast.

History before Christ came
catalogs our ancient blame;
as a race we've much to learn,
much to counter with our turn.

WOW, WHAT A TRIP!
REMEMBER THAT BY LOOKING BACK
AT OUR HISTORY WE CAN GAIN WISDOM TO LIVE TODAY.
I HOPE YOU'VE ENJOYED THIS SEARCH FOR
TREASURE AS MUCH AS I HAVE!

58

B.C. Timeline

Creation

4000 B.C.   3500 B.C.   3000 B.C.   2500 B.C.   2000 B.C.   1500 B.C.   1000 B.C.   500 B.C.   0

Europe

Italy
(Rome)

Greece

Turkey

Fertile Crescent

Israel

Egypt

Africa

China

India

Image Credits

creation-Green Bird-Luiz Pinheiro-Brazil
creation-yellow fish-Lavinia Marin-Bucharest, Romania
creation & Noah Poem-Nigel Clarke Lisburn-Antrim, United Kingdon
Creation-ringtailed Lemu--Noah critters were the meerkat, heron, vixen)
in-Silver Rat Snake-MadMaven/T.S. Heisele USA
Early Inhabitants-fork lightening-James Stratton-Nottingham, United Kingdom
Noah-Giraffe-Ferdi Colijn-Netherlands
Noah-Lions-Kirsten Pote-South Africa
Egypt-Gator-Sarah Brucker-Titusville, FL USA
Egypt-RamsesII (in dark with lights)-Leonardo Barbosa-Rio de Janeiro, Brazil
Egypt-Boat-Alexander Wallnoefer-Wallnoefer, Merano, Italy
Egypt-Philia Temple & Camel-Peter Caulfield-Halsted, Essex, United Kingdom
Egypt-Anubi-Davide Guglielmo-Italy
Jones-Stone Carving-getye1 (stock xchng user name)-Hungary
Hieroglyphics-carving-Matyn Jones-Penarth, Vale of Glamorgan, United Kingdom
Papyrus-Thad Zajdowicz-Rockville, MD USA
Covenant-Will/Testament-Shing Hei Ho-Melbourne, Australia
Joseph-wheat berries-Elke Rohn-United Kingdom
Joseph-dates-Lucyna Andrezejewska-Poland
Mummy-black jackal-Jon Bodsworth
Mummy-mummy-Joshua Sherurcij
Pyramids-Sridhar Vedala- Shanghai, China
Pyramids-canopic jars-Jon Bodsworth
Pyramids-Tut's Funeral Mask-Jon Bodsworth
Afterlife-Jon Bodsworth

James L-R: Solomon, Don Quixote, Robin Hood, Constantine, Elijah, George Washington, Cleopatra, Marco Polo, Napoleon, William Wallace.

Works Cited
Altman, Susan and Susan Lechner. Modern Rhymes About Ancient Times: Ancient Egypt. New York: Children's Press, 2001.
David, Rosalie. Growing Up in Ancient Egypt. Troll Associates: Eagle Books, 1994.
Giblin, James Cross. The Riddle of the Rosetta Stone: Key to Ancient Egypt. New York: Harper Trophy, 1990.
History Cards – Creation to Rome. Lancaster, PA: Veritas Press, 2005.
Isbouts, Jean-Pierre. The Biblical World: An Illustrated Atlas. Washington D.C.: The National Geographic, 2007.
Hart, George. Exploring the Past: Ancient Egypt. San Diego: Gulliver Books, 1988.
Millard, Dr. Anne and Patricia Vanags (Eds.). Children's Encyclopedia of History: First Civilizations to the fall of Rome. London: Usborne, 1985.
Reeves, Nicholas. Into the Mummy's Tomb: The Real-Life Discovery of Tutankhamun's Treasures. New York: Madison Press, 1992.
Wilson, Douglas and G. Tyler Fischer (Eds.). Omnibus I: Biblical and Classical Civilizations. Lancaster, PA: Veritas Press, 2005.